Administering a Negotiated Contract

by

Gilbert R. Weldy

NATIONAL ASSOCIATION OF SECONDARY SCHOOL PRINCIPALS
1904 Association Dr., Reston, Va. 22091

11-28-73

Copyright 1973

THE NATIONAL ASSOCIATION OF SECONDARY SCHOOL PRINCIPALS
1904 Association Dr., Reston, Va. 22091

ISBN 0-88210-046-7
Library of Congress Catalogue Card Number: 73-80782

$2 per copy. Twenty percent discount for 10 or more copies. Special rates for 25 or more copies available upon request. **Payment must accompany orders of five dollars or less.**

Table of Contents

Foreword

Among administrator associations the NASSP was the first to recognize the importance of professional negotiations. As a practical follow-up, several monographs have been published in recent years on the process and strategy of collective bargaining. Each focused on the critical role of the principal who for far too long had been conspicuous by his absence at the bargaining table. Others were cast in a decision maker's posture and altogether too frequently bargained away the rights of the building administrator. In so doing the scope, depth, and quality of the educational program were altered and in some cases damaged. The Association feels that it has had an influential hand on the national scene in correcting this situation, and in according the principal his rightful place in the sun.

This monograph raises another important issue, i.e., how does one live and work with a negotiated contract? To obtain a "firing line" perspective, an experienced principal was chosen for the assignment. Gilbert Weldy, a strong supporter of the NASSP, has impressive credentials in this field. For nearly a decade he has served as principal of the Niles Township North High School in Skokie, Illinois. A school of over 2,500 students in suburban Chicago, it has faced all of the problems that have plagued both schools and colleges in these turbulent times. His advice is sound and we commend the reading of this document to those who seek enlightenment, as well as stability, in the handling of a negotiated contract.

Owen B. Kiernan
Executive Secretary

Introduction

The life of the school principal has changed considerably in the last several years. Collective bargaining has become commonplace in our schools. The standby formulas used by principals in administering schools no longer seem to be dependable. The old theories, based on organizational flow charts, channels for decision making, hierarchical schemes, instructional leadership, and public relations have been replaced in many schools by rigid, comprehensive, prescriptive, and proscriptive master contracts which govern the principal's administrative style far beyond any theoretical administrative model he may have adopted.

No other development in the process of decision making and school governance has affected the work of the principal so much. The changes in professional relationships between teachers and administrators since the advent of collective bargaining have been cataclysmic.

Master contracts are comprehensive, written agreements that have the same effect as school board policies. Teacher groups have sought to broaden their contracts not only to include economic benefits but also to ensure their active participation in the decision making that affects their welfare and professional service. Teaching assignments, size of classes, number of preparations, and daily schedules are all brought to the bargaining table in the belief that decisions about them affect conditions of employment. Contracts have moved teachers, individually and collectively, into more active participation in the daily decision making provinces of the principal.

This monograph is not intended to herald a doomsday for principals. Rather it is intended to help principals find new formulas for administering schools under master contracts. This monograph will set forth the principles on which effective school administration can proceed, to the end that students will be better served in reaching their educational objectives.

Other NASSP publications on teacher collective bargaining accurately trace the development of the principal's role in this process. Beginning with Benjamin Epstein's booklet in 1965, which dealt with the principal's role, through the series of professional negotiations pamphlets by Epstein, Ackerly and Johnson, and Kramer, the issue of collective bargaining's effect on the principal has been thoroughly reviewed. (See bibliography.)

Questions like "What is Negotiable?" and "Where Does the Principal Belong?" have been answered by developments in school districts throughout the country and by legislative enactments in many states that have legitimized and formalized the collective bargaining relationship. "Professional associations" and "teachers unions" no longer espouse different aims or employ different tactics. In fact, they are merging. The number of school districts not having negotiated master contracts is shrinking.

For the purposes of this monograph, all references to *principal* are meant to include those who assist the principal in his administrative duties. These may be assistant principal, vice principals, coordinators, directors, or anyone at the building level who has administrative responsibility.

G.R.W.

I. Who Wants
the Principal?

TEACHER ORGANIZATIONS HAVE
REJECTED THE PRINCIPAL

Teacher organizations at one time may have wanted their administrators as advocates and spokesmen. At least some wanted them as consultants. If the principal was seen as the head teacher and the leader of teachers, he may have been welcomed to sit on their side of the negotiations table. Most teachers in more recent years, however, have not sought the principal as their advocate or spokesman and have had little regard for or confidence in him as a consultant. Teacher groups, as they have become more demanding and militant, have rejected administrators as being hostile to their interests. In their effort to have a target, teachers have often very effectively alienated the principal through pressure tactics which have disrupted schools, confused students, and interfered extensively with the administrative functions of the school.

Organizationally, principals have been gradually eased out of teacher associations. The American Federation of Teachers never has included principals in its membership, and the National

Education Association through many of its state affiliates has made principals unwelcome. They have disaffiliated administrator groups, have withdrawn services, and in general have been hostile to the interests of administrators. Principals have been excluded, therefore, from any role in negotiations on the side of teachers, either as active participants or advisers. NASSP as a professional organization for principals and other school administrators has severed its relationship with the National Education Association, as have other administrator groups.

BOARDS OF EDUCATION NEED THE PRINCIPAL

Boards of education at the same time are trying to retain management authority in their schools. Their one means of exercising authority and legal responsibilities is through the administrators they employ to carry out the goals of their school districts. In the adversary relationship of collective bargaining, school boards must have principals on "their side." A board of education, made up largely of laymen, is at a disadvantage in negotiating a comprehensive teacher contract, which in most school districts has far-reaching effects on the day-to-day operation of the schools—the very essence of the administrator's responsibility. A board must call upon administrators to develop its bargaining positions and to help reconcile differences with teachers without abdicating its control and without "giving away" the administration of the schools.

The board of education that recognizes its principals as leaders will want them to represent their interests at the bargaining table. Even if a board assumes responsibility for the table work in negotiations, or if it employs outside consultants as spokesmen, it will want building administrators nearby for the educational and operational issues. A contract negotiated without the direct involvement of principals, a school district's front-line leaders, will be imperfect at best.

PRINCIPALS FIND THEMSELVES

Principals during the first few years of board-teacher negotiations have been torn between their teachers and their governing boards. They truly have been the persons in the middle. At many conferences and workshops for school administrators during the last eight years, principals wrestled with this issue, split between loyalty to their teachers and accountability to their boards of education.

Principals of elementary schools and smaller secondary schools have had difficulty with this issue. Those principals who also teach, work in a close collegial relationship with their teachers. Teachers in these schools see their principals as protectors and advocates and expect them to support their bargaining position. Even in larger schools, many teachers looked to their principals for support.

The principal has to realize that when teachers negotiate the conditions of their employment, the conditions of employment for the principal are also being negotiated. What the teachers want in their contract will limit the principal's powers and subordinate his influence.

Contracts typically prescribe in detail how the principal and his administrative team are to carry out their duties in such areas as:

- conducting employment interviews
- supporting teachers in handling student discipline problems

- handling complaints from parents and students
- observing teachers, evaluating their performance, and conducting supervisory conferences
- dismissing teachers
- conducting grievance hearings
- transferring teachers
- assigning classes and scheduling teachers
- selecting teachers for promotion
- conducting faculty or departmental meetings.

In addition, specific prohibitions may be included in contracts to guarantee teachers that administrators will not:

- discriminate against them
- regulate their non-school activities
- influence them to join or not to join organizations representing teachers
- interfere with their efforts to seek employment elsewhere
- interfere with their academic freedom
- change students' grades
- interrupt teachers' classrooms except in emergencies
- observe or record a teacher's activities without his knowledge
- request substitute teachers to evaluate the regular teacher's preparation or plans
- be discourteous or disrespectful to teachers.

When items circumscribing the principal's role and defining his prerogatives are being negotiated by school boards and teacher groups, the principal had better be on the management negotiation team to represent himself. Some principals have been shocked and intimidated by contracts made by boards of education who had been subjected to several hours of highly persuasive teacher rhetoric at the negotiations table.

PRINCIPALS ARE THE KEY LEADERS IN BOTH MANAGEMENT AND PROFESSIONAL SENSES

During the years that the power-struggle between boards and teachers has ensued, principals have bemoaned their place as the unfortunate "person in the middle." Some principals have faced and resolved that dilemma. Where the principal belongs is clear. He is a key person on the management team and must declare allegiance to the board of education and the community by helping to carry out their goals. If he finds himself in consistent, absolute opposition to district goals, he should seek employment elsewhere.

Editor's note. A more complete exposition of the administrative role, the team concept, and the relationship of the team with boards of education will be found in the NASSP monograph, *Management Crisis: A Solution* and in the December, 1972, *NASSP Bulletin.*

II. How the Principal Prepares for Bargaining

PREPARING THE "PRINCIPAL'S PACKAGE"

Teacher organizations prepare for negotiations by assembling a package of their demands and proposals. Some are voluminous collections of every conceivable notion any teacher has for improving his working conditions—increasing his economic benefits or liberalizing his "rights" as a teacher. Such "comprehensive proposals" are developed during lengthy workshops by teacher committees gathering ideas, suggestions, and complaints from their colleagues. Some proposals are seriously presented for hard bargaining; some are in the "nice things to have if we can get them" category; and others are included for their nuisance or shock value to be traded away in the bargaining process.

Teacher proposals often are so staggering that boards simply take the stand that they must preserve their prerogatives and keep the district solvent. Boards frequently do not initiate new proposals themselves, except possibly a few economic offerings in the late stages of the bargaining. What proposals boards do present are usually modest and conservative, while most teacher proposals are ambitious and sometimes radical. Somewhere between, agreements are reached.

Principals should develop their "packages," too. Whether directly involved in bargaining or not, they should conduct their own workshops to prepare for bargaining. Their time will be spent well by doing the following:

▶ Review the current contract to identify clauses that have caused problems in its administration, including:

a. Ambiguous clauses that have been the source of conflicting interpretations requiring grievance action to clarify.

b. Inconsistencies in the contract, frequently the result of "zero-hour" bargaining when last-ditch efforts to wrap up an agreement are made. (Example: confusing and inconsistent language like "normal teaching schedule," "overall teaching schedule," "teacher's normal load," and "classroom teaching.")

c. Loose or time-consuming procedures for carrying out contractual rights.

d. Any clauses that would effectively block changes in school reorganization or program innovation that are anticipated by the administration. Such change may not have been contemplated when the contract was negotiated and may not have presented problems. (Example: unanticipated need to reduce staff as a result of dropping enrollment or budget cutbacks or a desire to use differentiated staffing.)

e. Any clause that interferes with the principal's normal prerogatives. (Example: not being able to change any "working condition" or "customary duty" without the agreement of the teachers' bargaining agent.)

f. Any gaps in the contract that raise issues over where authority lies.

g. Any clause that tends to favor certain teachers or certain groups of teachers. (Example: union members favored over non-union members.)

h. Any clause that does not recognize the administrator's right to evaluate and assign teachers according to their qualifications and abilities. (Example: most seniority provisions.)

▶ Review the contract for clauses that have *not* interfered with the administration of the school and at the same time have been fair and equitable for teachers. These should be included for "no change."

▶ Initiate proposals that administrators need for proper authority and control and for meaningful and efficient decision making on education issues. For example:

a. proposals to set up educational decision-making councils with parents, students, and teachers

b. proposals to provide school or departmental autonomy

c. proposals to simplify curriculum development procedures

d. proposals to clarify teachers' responsibilities for extra-class activities, supervision, non-teaching duties, definition of the school day

e. proposals to improve teacher evaluation procedures.

The board's negotiators should have a clear, articulate position on all issues and be ready with responses to all teacher demands, as well as to questions about their own proposals, including the "principal's package."

REACTION AND RESPONSE TO TEACHER PROPOSALS

Proposals presented by the teachers organization require an artful and careful analysis by the administrative team. Teacher proposals are predictable. They often have their origin in "lost" grievances, contract interpretation disputes, hurt feelings, and unrecognized "rights." The teacher proposals will also be borrowed heavily from neighboring districts where concessions have been won or precedents established.

The teachers' package of demands is usually available to the administrative team prior to the start of negotiations. The package is generally circulated among teachers as well, with the result that it is not much of a secret. Although some demands may be radical and some outrageous, all of them must be considered seriously even though the administrators may feel that some were presented with tongue in cheek.

A board position should be developed for each proposal after the proposals have been divided into economic and non-economic issues in the following general categories:

- accept without conditions
- accept with modifications
- accept with a "bargain"—look for a tradeoff
- hold and resist to late stages of negotiations for a "hard bargain"
- resist to the end—a strike issue
- non-negotiable—not appropriate for bargaining.

All teacher proposals should be analyzed for their cost and their effect on the educational program of the district. Some may seem not to have any relationship to student benefits, a criterion by which they should all be evaluated.

MANAGEMENT ISSUES IMPORTANT
TO THE PRINCIPAL

In preparing his package and in serving as active participant or consultant in negotiations, the principal should also guard his prerogatives as principal so that he can carry out his responsibilities without limitations or unnecessary constraints. The contract sets limits and establishes guidelines for certain administrative procedures. Furthermore, it tells teachers what to do if the principal violates any of their protections.

Most contracts remove actions for redress from the principal's hands after the first step in the grievance procedure. Therefore, the principal should exert as much influence as possible during the negotiations. The following list identifies some of the provisions that teachers have sought as rights but which, from management's perspective, are infringements upon necessary administrative authority:

- clauses which call for the election of principals by teachers and their recall if teachers disapprove of the principal's work
- specifications for procedures and conduct of employment interviews, notice to candidates, or prohibitions for the administrator in selecting teachers for employment
- provisions or clauses that are demeaning to administrators, such as the requirement that they be courteous and respectful to teachers, that they not discriminate because

of race or religion, or that they not ask embarrassing questions in employment interviews (All practices avoided by good administrators or those covered by law are not needed in teacher contracts.)

- clauses requiring administrators to report to teachers concerning actions or decisions that do not directly concern them
- clauses that unreasonably complicate the administrator's routine for carrying out supervisory duties
- clauses that allow teacher organization representatives to sit in on supervisory conferences or to receive summary reports of conferences, when the individual teacher has not requested such representation
- clauses that give teachers the right to grieve over the content and substance of their evaluations
- clauses that allow teachers to use the content of supervisory evaluations in the school or in the news media to attempt to embarrass or discredit administrators and supervisors
- clauses that require "concurrence" of the teacher bargaining unit before policies can be made or changed, or before educational decisions can be made
- clauses requiring the assignment or promotion of a teacher according to seniority, with no regard for qualifications or talent
- clauses calling for teachers to "concur" in their teaching assignment or schedule, or clauses allowing teachers to ask for changes in their assignment if they consider their assignment a "hardship"
- clauses placing unworkable restrictions on teacher assignments, such as arbitrary limits on the number of

different classrooms, arbitrary limits on the number of
preparations, and unreasonably limited class sizes

- clauses giving teachers the right to veto their own trans-
fers between departments or buildings
- clauses requiring laborious procedures for curriculum
development or innovation
- clauses limiting the principal's discretion to adjust the
daily schedule for special purposes or programs
- clauses that in any way interfere with the board of education's responsibility to adhere to the law or to respond
to community expectations in their schools.

Such a list of management issues should give principals some
pause, since many board-teacher contracts have already been
written with many of these clauses in them. Setting in order the
balance of power in some districts whose teachers have fought
hard on these issues is going to be most difficult and may lead to
major confrontations, but if the principal is to have the authority
to meet his responsibilities, provisions such as these must be
challenged and corrected.

The reader may be expecting to find a similar list of management issues that the principal should be attempting to get *into*
the contract. These won't be found here. Board-teacher contracts
are not bills of rights or job descriptions for administrator rights
and privileges. The administrator's rights and prerogatives are
to be found in state laws, board of education policies describing
his duties, and good management principles.

Editors' note. See bibliography for coverage of the principal's role during
negotiations.

III. Day-to-Day Administration of the Contract

WHAT THE CONTRACT MEANS TO THE PRINCIPAL

The contract is frequently referred to as the "teachers' contract." It seldom is called the "board's contract." Because principals have a daily association with teachers, occupy the same place of work, and have mutual responsibility for the immediate control, direction, and instruction of children, the principal's responsibility for daily contract administration has to be a greater concern for him than for administrators at any other level. Superintendents, their assistants, and school board members are several steps removed from this immediate daily contact and are more often involved in the legal and technical aspects of the contract or in directly representing the board of education in contract negotiations.

Once a contract has been negotiated and ratified by the teachers' group and the board of education, it becomes school district policy and supersedes any previous contrary board policy. The contract takes a place along with state law, court decisions, board policies, directives from superiors, regulations of state departments of education, accrediting association policies and criteria—not to mention unwritten codes and community expectations—as guides and controls for the principal in the performance of his duties.

In the eyes of a faculty, the contract is by far the most important of these guides, and many teachers will know its provisions minutely and expect them to be fulfilled to the letter. The contract is the teachers' document, written as a result of their efforts for fairer treatment, better working conditions, and improved economic benefits. Teachers see the contract as guaranteeing rights they have fought for, sacrificed for, and won. They believe that such rights would not have been given them except for their collective efforts and group solidarity. Teachers in schools with hard-won contracts will be seen carrying the contract with them. (Few teachers carry their state code books or board policy books around the schools.) Some teachers check the contract frequently, researching their rights and working conditions thoroughly.

A document so important to teachers has to be important to the principal. He should know its provisions as well as, if not better than, most of his teachers. If he has helped negotiate the contract, he will.

The principal should follow the contract in all his planning. He should accept it as the good-faith agreement of the teachers with the board. The bargaining may have been bitter, and a strike may have followed, but these disagreeable forerunners should not affect the principal's administration of the contract. The contract should be followed in spirit and intent as well as to the letter. The principal's success in having the support of teachers and reducing friction or disruption is dependent upon his willing use of the teachers' contract in administering his school.

SENSITIVE AREAS OF
CONTRACT ADMINISTRATION

Teachers as "Adversaries." Adversaries in any conflict want to win. The adversarial relationship that is created by collective bargaining frequently carries over into the day-to-day operations of the school, setting teachers and administrators at odds with each other in many work areas. The union or association representatives become "watch dogs" or "sentinels" for the teachers, looking for the administrator to step out of line (violate the contract).

Principals can easily become gun-shy, feeling that they are being watched, that their activities, communications, and decisions are being carefully monitored. In districts where teacher militancy is strongest, this impression may be more real than imagined. Most comprehensive contracts contain more than enough provisions so that, if a teacher is disgruntled, he can hang his complaint somewhere on the contract and bring a grievance. A convenient clause, used repeatedly, is one calling for courtesy in relationships.

In some cases this suspicious watchfulness borders on paranoia and keeps administrators off balance and may even affect their initiative and creativity. The principal can easily become intimidated, with the result that he may withhold decisions, procrastinate, or even abdicate rightful responsibilities.

The principal does *not* have use of the contract to reciprocate in kind, and shouldn't if he did. The contract is not an instrument typically carrying provisions for teacher responsibility, and it can't usually be used for discipline. Preferably, the principal uses his administrative prerogatives, if the contract has allowed him to retain any. His administrative authority plus his ability in management skills should be exercised in dealing with his "adversaries."

The relationship that develops between teachers and administrators from bargaining is extremely sensitive. The principal will have to seek ways of reconciliation, of gentle or not-so-gentle persuasion, of skillful compromise, in handling conflict situations which develop around the contract. He may be entirely unsuccessful in winning friends among teacher militants who see him as the target for their own frustrations and hostility, but he must establish some version of peaceful co-existence. He seldom can retaliate without further recrimination. His behavior is too public to allow for any kind of petty badgering that some teachers may engage in. He cannot assume a "hurt" posture and expect sympathy. Certainly he cannot lose his courage in the face of what may seem perpetual opposition and harrassment.

The principal *can*, without being collaborator or buddy, still command respect. He does so by being judicious, fair, democratic, and frank. He cannot be spiteful, vindictive, dishonest, or devious.

Most principals can take comfort in the fact that only a few teachers on their faculties will cause such distress. The danger is that the principal may, in responding to such hostility and suspicion from a few, allow his feelings to affect his relationship with the majority who will prefer and respond to more normal relationships.

"Put It in Writing." A contract is a legal document and requires a kind of formality and "legalese" that many principals

aren't accustomed to and don't care for. Most would prefer more dependence upon creative understanding, reached through open discussion. But the understanding which principals feel they have achieved may not be the same as what the teacher understands.

One principal who discussed (as called for by the contract) guidelines for scheduling thought he and the union representative had reached an understanding. When the guidelines were ready for publication to the faculty, the union representative took issue, wanting a slightly altered statement here, a bit more clarification there, and some underlining for emphasis.

The union representative was disappointed that the principal had not grasped the full substance of his own understanding. Fortunately, a few word changes resolved the misunderstanding. The lesson to be learned from such incidents is: *put it in writing.* Principals may feel that such formality is bothersome or even indicative of lack of trust and cooperation. On the contrary, such recording of agreements or summaries of discussions may be helpful in avoiding later misunderstandings and ill feeling. A good practice is to affix signatures to written understandings so that when agreements are reached through contractual procedures, everyone affected knows that the administration has consulted with the union and has its agreement. Otherwise, teachers are unsettled or must have communication from their union to know that a matter has properly followed contract procedures.

Joint statements by the principal and the union are appropriate and helpful when the subject is one which the contract calls for agreement or consultation with teachers. This in no way suggests that such joint communications should be used unless they are on subjects specifically required by the contract. A principal should not permit the teacher interest in participating in his decision making to intrude upon his proper administrative prerogatives even though the union or association may offer this "help" in obtaining teacher acceptance.

Contracts frequently call for agreement between the administration and teacher representatives in these areas of the school operation:

- scheduling the school day
- selecting textbooks
- changing curriculum
- making significant changes in the regular school program
- reaching temporary agreements outside of bargaining
- making exceptions to the contract
- planning the yearly school calendar.

In addition, many contracts require consultation* with teachers in such matters as:

- teacher assignments
- professional travel
- modifications in building facilities
- purchase of equipment
- changes in building policy
- evaluation conferences
- in-service activities, institutes, and faculty meetings.

In any such conferences leading to agreements or in any such consultations, the administrator should keep a careful record of all the discussion and deliberations. This record should include the date and time, the persons present, and the substance of the

* Care should be taken that this word is never "concurrence," which literally means that a teacher must agree before a decision is reached. "Concurrence" gives a teacher or the teachers' organization veto power over administrative actions or decisions.

discussion; and, if there was an agreement or decision reached, it should be recorded with exact wording and signatures of those responsible for each "side." In some cases, when the matter is of considerable importance, a professional stenographer may be used or even a tape recorder.

No matter how much the administrator and teachers may wish to depend on good will and mutual trust, a careful record of meetings on contractual matters is imperative. The good will you may have can be destroyed by one occasion where parties to a "friendly agreement" remember the discussion differently. The record which is made should be reviewed at the earliest opportunity by both sides to confirm that this is, in fact, what both parties thought had transpired. If the record is made in a series of meetings, the "minutes" can be approved at each succeeding meeting.

Sole Bargaining Agents. Another area that may be a sensitive one is the effort by unions or associations, as the sole recognized bargaining agents for teachers, to extend their influence and activity into areas that are not specifically called for by the contract. The fact that a teacher group has sole bargaining rights does not automatically give it the right to act in ways that are not agreed upon in the contract, including such areas as:

- appointing their members to standing faculty committees
- sitting in on administrative conferences or departmental meetings
- sitting in on evaluation conferences with teachers
- appointing members to policy-making groups
- attempting to exclude non-member teachers from participating in committees or policy-making groups
- interfering with or pre-empting administrative communications.

Particularly, it would be harmful to have teacher groups establish these practices by precedent when the board of education has resisted these demands at the bargaining table. A board's resistance to such pressures is considerably weakened when the teacher bargainers proclaim: "We're already doing that now! What's the problem?"

Teacher Evaluation. An area that has complicated principals' lives under contracts is teacher evaluation. Previously, teachers have had little or nothing to say about how they were evaluated or even what the criteria were to be. In many schools, they were literally at the mercy of whatever administrative philosophy or procedure the principal and his assistants happened to use. Teacher evaluation, principals must admit, is a responsibility which prior to negotiations was done very poorly in many situations. The great lengths that teachers have gone to in bargaining to spell out every aspect of how administrators evaluate their service is ample evidence that this is a grave concern of teachers. Typically, contracts include specifications on these aspects of teacher evaluation:

- procedures for establishing the criteria for an evaluation system and their regular review
- requirements for announcing visits to classes
- prohibitions on the use of mechanical devices or recording equipment
- requirements that the teacher be fully aware that he is being observed and evaluated
- requirements for the length and frequency of observations
- requirements for conferences before and after visits
- requirements and format for written observation reports

- provisions for maintenance of the teachers' file of his record of service
- provisions for the teacher to disagree with or dispute the substance of his evaluation
- prohibitions against having any unauthorized persons attempt to provide evaluation of the teacher's service
- careful procedures for pointing out deficiencies, making suggestions for improvement, assisting the teacher in overcoming deficiencies
- procedures for handling complaints against teachers
- review of dismissal decisions.

The effect of such detailed contractual provisions causes principals to give much more attention to the procedures for teacher evaluation than ever before. Principals are bound to be more thorough and more cautious in their supervisory activities. Another effect may well be that the principal completely withdraws from any supervisory activities in the face of such requirements.

For the teachers, an effect not so desirable is that they may feel, under such rigorous, formalized procedures, more threatened and more intimidated by observation and evaluation than ever before. There is hardly any way that a principal can pose as one whose primary interest is in improvement of instruction when the two-day notice of the visit, pre-visitation conference, the visit, the post-visit evaluation conference, and the written evaluation, officially filed, all spell for the teacher a formal, imposing, threatening critique that could be used to downgrade him or even to dismiss him.

Teachers pay much closer attention to the substance of these evaluation statements, are more inclined to seek word changes, or try to influence the evaluator, to ensure that there is no content that might be used against them. The insecure probationary teacher may panic and take issue with even the mildest criticism or suggestion even in the context of an otherwise very complimentary appraisal.

The effect of this attitude toward evaluation is two-fold for the principal. Either he escapes from the responsibility of writing honest, fair appraisals and writes bland, noncommittal, mildly complimentary reports—or he over-reacts by withholding praise in any instance when he feels that his documentation may be needed in a troublesome re-appointment decision. Dismissal cases that are based on the principal's supervisory reports can present some dilemma for those who review the case through the grievance procedure, because any favorable comment will be used to support the teacher's case—*against* the principal who wrote it and recommended the dismissal.

Most contract requirements have not provided the principal with any assistance in his efforts to improve instruction through the usual supervisory techniques. His genuine interest in each teacher will have to show clearly. His concern for the teacher's success will have to be sincere. His knowledge of instructional techniques must be thorough; his perception of problems, accurate. His suggestions will have to be specific and helpful, their outcome fruitful. The principal's role as a supervisor under the contract may not be easier, but it has to be better.

Principals can be reassured by the results of several studies of teacher attitudes toward supervision, which indicate teacher preference for the principal as the person who should supervise their teaching. A 1969 NEA Research Bulletin reports a survey of 235 school systems in which 96.6 percent of the teachers preferred the principal as their evaluator, in preference over supervisors, department chairmen, or other teachers.

The Effect of the Teachers' Contract on Students and Parents.
Negotiators are not always as sensitive as they should be to
the effect that some of the agreements will have on the welfare
and wishes of students and parents. Contracts affect students
and parents too, sometimes taking away their discretion, their
options, or maybe even their rights. The contract can interject
itself into areas where the principal is dealing with students and
parents, such as:

- provisions that make grades the final responsibility of
  teachers with no provision for review or for appeal
- requirements that the administration always support
  teachers in disciplinary actions—or, in some contracts,
  provisions for giving teachers final authority to exclude
  students from their classes
- rigid class size limits or limits on total student load that
  have the effect of keeping students out of classes or
  blocking program or schedule changes that would be
  desirable for a student
- procedures for handling complaints from students and
  parents that have the tendency to discourage meaningful
  dialogue with teachers on legitimate concerns or problems
- strong "academic freedom" clauses that are used for
  license by teachers to alter curriculum, depart from
  normal instructional procedures, dismiss classes, or ig-
  nore attendance requirements
- teacher "rights" provisions that allow teachers to be
  absent from the school building during "unassigned"
  time; to choose not to attend meetings or to neglect to
  stay after school to help students; to disclaim any responsibility for students outside the classroom; or to

decline the usual supervisory responsibilities for students' extracurricular activities.

Principals may find themselves confronted by students and parents whose requests or complaints may be quite legitimate. When the teacher contract prevents an accommodation for the student that would really be in his best interests, the principal's position is a weak one. A statement like "I'm sorry, but our teacher contract does not allow that" rarely satisfies. Students and parents can easily wonder who the schools are for, and the principal finds himself neatly sandwiched in-between again.

ADMINISTRATION OF GRIEVANCE PROCEDURES

Grievance procedures are a part of virtually every negotiated contract for teachers. The grievance is generally defined as any violation, mis-application, or misinterpretation of the contract. Grievance definitions may also extend to written board of education policies or even to written administrative procedures, but such liberal interpretations should be avoided.

The principal is almost always the first step in the grievance procedure. Grievance steps at the principal's level allow for informal resolution of complaints with no written documentation either of the complaint or of the resolution. Most grievances are settled in this manner if the principal makes an honest, good faith effort to resolve differences or to interpret the contract objectively. The principal who views grievances as challenges to his administrative authority or who views them as intentional harrassment will probably experience considerable discomfort with grievances.

On the other hand, if the principal can view the grievance as an honest effort by a teacher or the teacher's organization to find redress for a wrong or to get an interpretation of the contract, he will be able to use the orderly processes of the grievance procedure to resolve differences or to settle complaints amicably. The grievance procedure ensures a teacher of due processes in the protection of his rights under the contract. The principal cannot with impunity interfere with or obstruct this process in any way.

The principal must see the grievance machinery as a necessary part of the contract, which is usually an imperfect instrument, negotiated and written by educators, not primarily by lawyers. The contract is subject to varying interpretations, particularly by those who were not involved in the negotiations and were not aware of the development of an agreement and its intent. Such variations of interpretation require a grievance procedure to clear up disagreements and establish precedents for future contractual relationships and for future negotiations.

An example of a grievance of interpretation might occur in a contract which says: "A maximum of two percent of the instructional staff may be granted sabbatical leave in any given school year." A school board might claim that this clause does not guarantee any leaves, that the key word is *may*. Teachers, on the other hand, may have understood they were getting guaranteed sabbaticals for two percent of the faculty each year.

Grievance procedures also are needed because imperfect contracts are administered by fallible administrators. Human errors may need correction, particularly if someone has been injured as a result. Such grievances are usually brought because of an administrator's failure to know the contract thoroughly or because of a conflict generating hard feelings. The grievance procedure could, under these circumstances, be used to retaliate against or to embarrass an administrator. Grievances are typically the direct result of administrative decision or behavior.

With this exposition on grievances, it should be apparent to principals that grievance machinery in our schools is a fact of administrative life and must be accepted and used as one of his regular administrative procedures.

The principal can live with grievance procedures if he follows these guidelines:

- ▶ Know the contract minutely; follow its provisions meticulously.
- ▶ If there are difficulties in adhering to the contract, or if exceptions are needed in order to serve students better, consult with teacher representatives to see if the variation may be allowed. Most contracts carry provisions for temporary agreements.
- ▶ Welcome questions of interpretation of the contract from teachers. Establish yourself as an expert on the contract who can answer questions with confidence and render opinions with authority. Responses to teachers' questions should be prompt and clear.
- ▶ The principal should follow all procedures willingly. He should not try to shortcut or circumvent the established grievance procedures, nor should he overtly or even inadvertently squelch grievance action by teachers.
- ▶ Teachers and their representatives should make it clear to the principal when they are approaching him on a grievance. The principal may not view every discussion of a complaint or a contractual question as a grievance, but the teacher may actually have that in mind. The principal may not use appropriate procedures or meet

his time limits for responding if he does not understand a discussion to be an informal grievance hearing. He should simply ask: "Are we hearing a grievance? May we consider this the informal conference?" The teacher may or may not have the representation he desires; therefore, the principal must be certain of his ground and not assume that the conference is something that it is not. This may not seem as though it should be a problem but in schools with little experience with grievance machinery, teachers may be reluctant to use the grievance, and principals may prefer not to acknowledge it.

▶ Efforts should always be made first to resolve questions informally. Discussions at that stage are usually more friendly and not so legalistic. Resolution will be easier in face-to-face efforts to get parties to understand each other and to discuss fine points of interpretation in the contract. Informal resolution is preferable also because lengthy written documentation and responses are not necessary. Writing answers to grievances requires extensive study of the contract and careful composition.

▶ The grievance conference or hearing should be set at a time convenient to all participants with sufficient time allowed. Contracts may provide substitutes for teachers involved in grievance hearings. The principal should be sure, if he knows the substance of the complaint and the parties involved, to have them all there. Teacher representatives, witnesses, administrators, students, and even parents may be involved. If all persons involved are not available, the hearing should be set for a more suitable time.

▶ The principal should examine all circumstances, consult

any authority available, and take as much time as provided by the contract before responding to the grievance. His interpretation should be the best he is capable of rendering. Even so, it may be appealed to the next level, typically the superintendent or the assistant superintendent for personnel.

▶ The decision should be based on precise interpretation of the contract. A principal does not "make points" by "settling at any price" all grievances at his level. This practice may in fact be dangerous, leading him to allow contract interpretations that were never intended by the board's negotiators and that are contradictory to grievance decisions in other schools in the district.

▶ Written grievance findings and decisions should be prepared with utmost care. Documentation must be thorough. Language should be clear and concise. If the principal feels inadequate in this regard, he should seek help from a colleague. The principal cannot render an inaccurate or prejudiced judgment, carelessly composed. His written document will be used by the superintendent, probably by the board of education, and possibly even by an independent arbiter or the courts. A poorly prepared written grievance decision can be a serious reflection on the principal's competency.

▶ The principal should feel free to seek the counsel of his colleagues, the school attorney, members of the board's negotiating team, and especially his superintendent. If the superintendent is the next step in the grievance procedure, the principal may like to know that his superintendent agrees with his interpretation or his action. If the principal knows the contract, researches the issues thoroughly, and gets the best advice he can, he should be able to anticipate that the superintendent will support his position. Teachers may see this as "stacking the deck" against them, but there is nothing irregular in the principal's use of such procedures. Grievances may be thoroughly discussed by the superintendent and the board while they are still at the principal's level. The result may be, of course, that complaints unresolved at the principal's level will be appealed and unresolved through all the steps of the grievance procedure. Superintendents will generally want to support principals, and boards will want to support their superintendents.

▶ Principals should not view decisions on grievances as won or lost, even though teacher organizations may cite decisions favorable to teachers as victories for their organization.

▶ The principal must help his assistants and other supervisors of teachers to accept grievance decisions gracefully. The principal may not be able to decide a grievance in support of his administrative colleagues. Their behavior or their decisions may have been at fault. As much as the principal wants to support his fellow administrators, he owes support to teachers also—and is obligated to respect the integrity of the contract. His decision must be the fairest and most impartial interpretation of the contract that he can render.

▶ The principal, at the same time, must be able to accept reversals of his decisions by the superintendent. Although grievance procedures are legal guarantees of rights, they are not as formal as the courts. New information or insights may be introduced at the superintendent's level and could change a decision. The principal should not be hurt or feel rebuffed.

Principals can use grievance procedures as an effective tool of administration. They should accept them as an orderly process for correcting injurious acts or bringing redress for violations of the contract.

RELATING TO TEACHERS UNDER THE CONTRACT

Little needs to be offered here to demonstrate that teacher organizations have become more militant. Principals in service over the past 10 years know all about teacher militancy. The debate will rage on, over whether this aggressive teacher behavior will serve students better or worse.

Such changed relationships may be irrevocable in some schools because teachers depend so much on their organizations and turn to them for every request, thereby diminishing the principal's influence. At least the attitude described requires a different style of administration and a different philosophy of management.

IV. Problems with Administrator-Teacher Roles Under the Contract

ADMINISTRATORS IN THE BARGAINING UNIT

Administrators are not usually welcome in the bargaining unit in schools with strong master contracts. However, the wedge that negotiations has driven between principals and teacher groups has not always split roles as neatly as good management will require.

The most troublesome dilemma is for the person who shares administrative and teaching duties, such as department chairmen, area coordinators, or teaching principals. Such positions have become increasingly untenable under master contracts. Some contracts have made the role of such teacher–supervisors intolerable by making conditions of their employment (such as pay, duties, and authority) subjects for bargaining. Boards of education have objected to the inclusion of such subjects in bargaining, but when the teacher-supervisor is a long-standing, dues-paying member, the organization will try to represent him. In some instances, teacher groups have even attempted to represent principals. When administrative salaries are tied to teacher salaries, this representation occurs even when it is not intended.

The illogic of this arrangement is under close scrutiny most everywhere it exists. The questions are:

- Can the same person be both a supervisor of teachers and an ally with teachers in a bargaining unit?
- Where are the loyalties of the person in this position?
- In conflict situations, is the supervisor under the direction of the board and superintendent or is he providing a cushion for the teacher?
- Who controls the supervisor—the board or the teachers?
- How can a bargaining unit represent one member in a grievance against another?
- What is the motive of the teachers group in holding onto the supervisor?
- Do they feel that he needs representation and that they can provide it more effectively than he can for himself?
- Why do supervisors accept and perpetuate this cozy arrangement?

The answers to these questions may vary from school to school, and the solutions may vary as well. Much depends upon the relationships between the school board and the teachers. If bargaining is low key and friendly and if the contract is limited in its scope and influence, a school may be able to endure with department chairmen or even principals in the bargaining unit, but probably not for long. The nature and extent of the duties the teacher–supervisors perform is significant. If they evaluate teachers; help make decisions for hiring, firing, or promotion; if they make teacher assignments; if they control a budget—the likelihood that they should remain comfortably in any bargaining unit is remote.

Boards of education that are concerned about their control of schools and about their ability to have policy decisions implemented have cleared up this confusion by refusing to allow teacher groups to negotiate for anyone who has administrative or supervisory responsibilities. This separation of the "teachers' teacher" from the bargaining unit has been painful in many schools, but altogether logical and necessary.

In one school district, the place of the department chairman (a teacher who supervised other teachers) became part of the power struggle, and the only way the struggle could be resolved was by eliminating the position of department chairman and establishing a new management structure that clearly separated the functions of teacher and administrator.

This painful wrenching of teacher supervisors from the bargaining unit can best be accomplished by school boards who recognize the need to establish working conditions, economic benefits, and authority commensurate with responsibility for the principal and his management team. A board of education—which needs control and authority—will need a management team that is loyal and supportive and believes in the same objectives for the school. The goal, of course, should be that schools serve educational purposes for children—not teachers, administrators, or the board of education.

CLARIFYING THE ADMINISTRATOR-TEACHER ROLES

During a period of adjustment to new roles and new relationships, teachers and principals often are in conflict about what is an "administrative duty" or a "teacher's duty." Remember that the thrust of much of the negotiations from the teacher point of view has been to attempt to "professionalize" the role of the teacher by freeing him from any tasks which are regarded as "administrative" or as clerical, custodial, housekeeping, routine, or by whatever definition are "sub-professional." As a result of such teacher efforts, schools have employed clerks, aides, monitors, supervisors, and para-professionals to assume these duties. Teacher organizations have been most protective in reserving for teachers what they consider to be responsibilities of the professional teacher.

One strange twist of this reasoning by teachers is their rejection of duties that they consider to be "administrative"—whether teachers are to perform such tasks as receive supplies, store equipment, help keep inventory, prepare purchase orders, lock up classrooms, schedule facilities, distribute textbooks, or handle instructional equipment. It is interesting that some teachers have taken the position that these duties are beneath the professional level of the teacher's expertise—but quite appropriate for administrators.

The problem for the administrator under these arrangements is that most schools do not have a clearly defined "job description" for teachers. Such sets of duties and responsibilities are not typically found in negotiated contracts, and they are missing from or only implied in board of education policies. Such lack of agreement and understanding complicates the relationships that principals have with teachers. Gaps appear between what needs to be done in a school and what each bargaining group (teachers, clerks, custodians, and possibly even administrators) accepts as its rightful responsibilities.

Schools need to supplement their contracts with clear policies on what a teacher's responsibilities are. The contract spells out only what they are not. Boards of education will be wiser to have these duties established in board policy rather than attempt to negotiate them at the bargaining table. Principals working within such policies will smooth out some of the troublesome relationships that result when competing groups all try to improve their working conditions, circumscribing and delimiting their roles.

What are a teacher's responsibilities? Theoretically, teachers spend four years in college learning the teacher's role. Policies on teachers' responsibilities are not in textbooks on how to teach. This is legitimately where the teacher's professional training and expertise take over. As a result of teacher negotiations, however, there are a good many areas of difference about certain aspects of the teacher's responsibilities, as well as many misconceptions about academic freedom and professional autonomy.

For example, all of the following traditional aspects of the teacher's role have been challenged and questioned in the process of negotiations. These *are* legitimate, necessary duties of teachers and cannot and should not be delegated to others or left undone at the discretion of the teacher.

- Take and record attendance in classes.
- Assign and record grades on the basis of progress toward course objectives.
- Supervise and attend to student misbehavior when it occurs in the teacher's presence in the hallways, cafeterias, washrooms, or grounds.
- Care and be responsible for the security of instructional equipment.

- Teach toward the established agreed-upon objectives of the course assigned. (Course objectives should be written; materials lists, published.)
- Meet and hold classes for the duration of the assigned time.
- Respond to legitimate concerns of students and parents about student progress.
- Furnish data for enrollments, class sizes, and other administrative information.
- Serve on all-school welfare and planning committees.
- Participate in faculty deliberations and decision making on general school policies.
- Meet with students, parents, and administrators on advisory committees.
- Attend and supervise reasonable extracurricular activities.

Other professional duties of teachers that in most schools remain unquestioned but should be spelled out in school policy are these:

- Assist in development of course objectives and goals.
- Assist in establishing criteria for selection of textbooks and other instructional materials.
- Participate in selection of textbooks and other teaching materials and equipment.
- Assist in development of criteria and instruments of course (curriculum) evaluation.
- Adaptation of curriculum materials and course objectives to agreed-upon program priorities and to the needs of students assigned.
- Assist with coordination of the teacher's subject area with other programs in the school.

- Articulate goals, content, and material with programs in elementary schools and colleges.
- Participate in general curriculum planning.
- Prepare data for the annual budget proposal.
- Prepare purchase orders; record purchases; receive supplies and equipment.
- Report damage, loss, theft, or depreciation of equipment, furniture, or fixtures.
- Accept all students assigned within contract limits, and work with individual students who need assistance.
- Supervise open labs, classrooms, activity areas, study halls, and resource centers.
- Serve on committees to plan professional leaves, field trips, special programs, large group presentations.
- Screen and select students for departmental awards, honor societies, scholarships.
- Conduct studies and research, prepare data, and complete reports for accrediting associations, state departments of education, federal agencies, and, of course, for the local district.
- Prepare course descriptions or other data needed to communicate the nature of program offerings for student registration.
- Respond to administrative requests for information or opinions.
- Attend departmental and all-school faculty meetings.
- Keep fair and reasonable discipline in the classroom.

This list is not meant to be exhaustive, only illustrative. There should never be any question or conflict about what a teacher's duties are if such statements are adopted by a board of education and appear in published policies.

Just as important is careful delineation and clear understanding of what the administrator's duties are. Teachers should know what they can expect of their administrators. The following duties are clearly administrative and are usually considered "in line" on the management chart with authority leading directly from the school board.

- Direct and coordinate all planning and program development.
- Oversee the development of clear purposes and objectives for all programs.
- Assist in developing alternative plans for meeting program objectives.
- Assist in selecting priorities among alternative plans and programs.
- Direct the development of criteria for evaluation of programs.
- Recruit, screen, and select members of the professional and support staff.
- Supervise, evaluate, and recommend for re-appointment or dismissal all professional and support staff.
- Make assignments and develop schedules for all staff.
- Collect data and prepare and justify the annual budget requests for the department or school.
- Direct all activities for selection of instructional materials, equipment, and supplies.
- Plan instructional facilities.
- Establish procedures for inventory and security.
- Prepare information and set procedures for student registration and scheduling.
- Organize all routines necessary for maintenance, safety, security, discipline, attendance, and welfare of students.

- Prepare reports of status of all school programs and procedures for district, board of education, state, or federal use.
- Provide leadership and direction for all aspects of the school or departmental operation.
- Provide program of in-service staff development, including induction and orientation of new staff members.
- Serve as representative and spokesman of the school with community groups, parent clubs, district administrative bodies, and with the board of education.

Similar lists of duties should be developed for all classifications of school staff, particularly those who serve in a para-professional role, working in close association with teachers. Teacher assistants, aides, lay readers, lay supervisors, resource center or lab aides, should all have their duties clearly defined so that there is no conflict in role definition or misunderstanding or disagreement about who is responsible for every aspect of a school program.

Add to these effects of negotiations, the effect of communities and governmental units' emphasis on accountability and productivity, and the separation of the teacher and administrator role is more distinct. Communities through their boards of education, and boards through their administrators are holding educators accountable for the product of the schools. They demand fiscal responsibility. They look for cost effectiveness.

INVOLVING TEACHERS IN ADMINISTRATIVE PROBLEM SOLVING

Establishing clear definitions of duties for teachers and administrators does not mean that each group does not need, depend upon, or even relate to the other. Clarification of roles should serve to improve communication, to relieve tension, to facilitate the task, and to render more defensible decisions.

The National Association of Secondary School Principals in its publications and policy statements has consistently advocated that teachers participate in solving the problems of education. Teacher opinions are most valuable in such areas as curriculum, organization for instruction, textbook selection, student activities, in-service training, auxiliary services, and discipline of students. NASSP has emphasized that discussions and decisions on these purely professional problems cannot be considered in an atmosphere characteristic of the bargaining table. In the need to solve professional problems, principals and teachers should not be adversaries. Their interests are the same. The principal should establish communication channels, internal organization, and decision-making councils that ensure teacher participation—not perfunctory, meaningless rubber-stamping—but true involvement where their professional expertise is valued and used!

The disharmony that frequently emanates from the collective bargaining relationship should not impair the principal's ability to work cooperatively with teachers in seeking professional solutions to problems.

V. Preparing Principals for Contract Administration

THE OFFICE OF THE PRINCIPAL— UNDER NEW MANAGEMENT

If principals recognize themselves as leaders in management, and furthermore acknowledge that their role has changed, they should be ready to seek strategies and skills to cope successfully with contract administration.

New philosophies of management, bringing successful techniques of business to education, are providing school principals with many of the strategies that will enable them to continue to exercise leadership in their schools. Management by objectives and PPBS (program, planning, and budgeting systems) are sophisticated systems that help give credibility to management as a profession. School principals as professional administrators occupy a critical position in American education, one that deserves the best level of performance principals can attain.

SKILLS THE PRINCIPAL WILL NEED

The changing roles that result from negotiated contracts call for different administrative strategies and techniques. The administrator working under provisions of a master contract should remember that the contract is not the source of his management rights. Administrators retain all the management rights that have not been specifically bargained away in the contract. Bargaining seldom gets anything for management; it usually gives authority and discretionary powers away. Administrators must use the authority that remains invested in their position and develop the competencies to complement that authority.

The administrator will need skill in group processes. He must have the ability to meet with his professional staff, capitalize on their talents, solicit their ideas, compromise differences, and reach creative, supportable decisions. The professional staff must be involved in planning under the administrator's direction. The administrator who does not have expertise in the subject area he supervises should not pretend expertise or try to make decisions alone when he needs professional assistance or advice. He must use his administrative skills to make the school responsive to the community. Programs under his direction should promote goals that the community supports and will pay for.

The administrator will have to be able to set up procedures and routines that assure his teachers that their needs for instructional programs will be promptly and adequately supported. This includes not only physical facilities, supplies, textbooks, and equipment, but also clerical services, information, and decisions when they are needed. The administrator should be the most important support person for teachers. He should be virtually indispensable to teachers. He should remove obstacles, facilitate work, and eliminate irritants.

The administrator should be prompt in getting answers to questions, responding to requests, supplying a need, or anticipating a problem.

The administrator will need skills in human relations. He may be feared and resented because of the attitude that teachers develop when their organization enters the adversary relationships of collective bargaining. He should show clearly and openly that he cares for people, both teachers and students. He should be fair in making assignments. He should promote a relationship with his teachers that demonstrates to them their value as contributing professionals. He should show appreciation and give credit where it is due. He should be able to absorb hostility and not retaliate. He must be an accepting, feeling, caring human being. He should be tactful and considerate. His mind should be open.

The administrator should know how to organize the activities and services of his department or program to expedite the work to be done. He should develop simple, convenient, workable procedures. He should have numerous communication channels open both ways. He should consider carefully when to consult, when to send written memos, when to call meetings. He should be protective and considerate of teachers' professional time.

The administrator can and should continue to be a leader. He should work harder, be more conscientious, and set the pace for his teaching group. He should at all times be willing to set the example for what he expects of his teachers.

The administrator in his new role must be sure of his ground and certain that his teachers understand his function. He must adhere to master contract provisions and not try to circumvent them for his own purposes. The contract must be followed in good faith.

The administrator must be more sensitive than ever before to human rights, more specifically to teacher rights, that may or may not be delineated in the negotiated contract. More time and attention must be given to the equity of assignments, the fairness of decisions, and the quality of his evaluations. Administrators cannot with impunity expect to be arbitrary or willful, unmindful of how their decisions and actions affect teachers and students. His goal, of course, must be that programs and activities of his school serve to benefit students and promote the goals of the community for its schools.

CONCLUSION

The principal's leadership has not diminished as a result of collective bargaining of master contracts. He need not be threatened or intimidated into submission or inactivity. His style must change because the role and the rules have changed. Weak administration under strong master contracts creates a power imbalance, causing confusion and inertia. Teachers, students, and community members still expect and respect good sound leadership. They will all be looking toward the principal to provide it.

Bibliography

1. Ackerly, Robert and Johnson, W. Stanfield. *Critical Issues in Negotiations Legislation.* Washington, D.C.: National Association of Secondary School Principals, 1969.
2. Angell, George W. "Grievance Procedures Under Collective Bargaining: Boon or Burden?" *Phi Delta Kappan,* April 1972.
3. Baer, Walter E. *Grievance Handling, 101 Guides for Supervisors.* American Management Associates, Inc., 1970, pp. 289.
4. Epstein, Benjamin. *The Principal's Role in Collective Negotiations Between Teachers and School Boards.* Washington, D.C.: National Association of Secondary School Principals, 1965.
5. Epstein, Benjamin. *What Is Negotiable?* Washington, D.C.: National Association of Secondary School Principals, 1969.
6. "Evaluation of Teacher Competence." *NEA Research Bulletin.* Oct. 1969, pp. 67–75.
7. Kramer, Louis I. *Principals and Grievance Procedures.* Washington, D.C.: National Association of Secondary School Principals, 1969.
8. National Association of Secondary School Principals. *Management Crisis: A Solution.* Washington, D.C.: NASSP, 1971.
9. National Association of Secondary School Principals. "The Principal and PPBS." *The Bulletin of the NASSP,* Vol. 56, No. 366, Oct. 1972.
10. National Association of Secondary School Principals. *The Bulletin of the NASSP.* Vol. 55, No. 359, Dec. 1971.
11. National Commission for the Defense of Democracy through Education. "Taking the Grief out of Grievances in Public School Systems." Washington, D.C.: National Education Association, 1961.
12. Odiorne, George S. *Management by Objectives, A System of Managerial Leadership.* New York: Pitman Publishing Co., 1972, p. 204.
13. Perry, Charles R. and Wildman, Wesley A. *The Impact of Negotiations in Public Education. The Evidence from the Schools.* Worthington, Ohio: Charles A. Jones Publishing Co., 1970, p. 254.